LXXXX
COLLECTED POEMS

LXXXX
COLLECTED POEMS

Lewis Kornfeld

Copyright © 2006 by Lewis Kornfeld.

ISBN: Hardcover   1-4257-2748-4
          Softcover   1-4257-1749-7

All rights reserved. No part of this book may be reproduced or transmitted in any form or by any means, electronic or mechanical, including photocopying, recording, or by any information storage and retrieval system, without permission in writing from the copyright owner.

This book was printed in the United States of America.

To order additional copies of this book, contact:
Xlibris Corporation
1-888-795-4274
www.Xlibris.com
Orders@Xlibris.com
34360

Other books by Lewis Kornfeld

NOVELS

The Fielder Heart
A Female Companion
The Love Gene
Moore's Law
Agent Orange

•

SHORT STORIES

The Pheromone Factor

•

ADVERTISING / MARKETING

To Catch a Mouse, Make a Noise Like a Cheese.

CONTENTS

Aarpeggio 13
Add Libs 14
a/k/a 15
Aperçu 16
Appearances 17
Avunc 18
Bang Lore 19
Breathless 20
Bruises 21
Cicerone 22
Cleavage 23
Closet Drama 24
Consumation 25
Convergence 26
Corporeality 27
Crazy Lady 28
Cygneture 29
Dispositions 30
Distance 31
Dobson's Choice 32
Endgame 33
Entr'acte 34
Evanescence 36
Fonetics 37
For Joe at 77 38
F-Stop 39
Genius Thoughts 40
Giggles 41
Grand Dragon 42
Harliquessence 43
Hegira 44
Idol Thoughts 45
Illuminatus 47
Inamorata 48
Indiana 49
Investiture 50

Junction	51
Kinethics	52
Last Rites	53
Leavings	54
Lettitude	55
Life or Death	56
Little hitler	58
Lou	59
Love-in	60
Made Things	61
Manhattan Serenade	62
Matter Natter	63
Messy Antics	64
Meum et Tuum	65
Mind's Eye	66
Mishima	67
Miss Tique	68
Muni Bonds	69
Nachtmusik	70
Obiter Dicta	71
On State Street	72
Outgrowth	73
Past Imperfect	74
Pathology	75
Picture Perfect	76
Position Paper	78
Prime Time	79
Psalmsung 23	80
Quantum Leap	82
Quarterly Report	83
Quintessence	84
Quotidian	85
Summation	86
Rondo	87
Seascape	88
Second Coming	89
Sequence	90
Skyfall	91
Stardom	92

Stet	93
Streamlines	94
String Theory	95
Ten O'clock News	96
The Look	97
Tidings	98
Time Frame	99
Timelines	100
Trinity	101
Ventilation	102
Wasteland?	103
Weekdaze	104
Western-449	105
Whispers	106
Zero-Sum	107

Ninety Robins

Surprised? Don't be. I've been writing poetry since the 1930s. These poems were written during the seventy-one years beginning with my University of Denver days (1935-1941), my pre-war brief stint as a reporter for Rocky Mountain News, through and beyond my life as a businessman at RadioShack Corporation (1948-2003). My two longest periods of poetic silence were during Marine Corps service in WWII and my eventual writing (1982-2006) of seven books of prose. Although I didn't hawk my verses to publishers, I kept on scribbling, stashing them away in a plastic bag that weighed six pounds when I recovered it from a dark, high clothes-closet shelf in early 2005 to see if any might be worth including in a book with my newer compositions.

The need for revision of poems past proved to be substantial, but it was a genuine pleasure to review and rewrite many of them; imagine, if you will, revisiting love letters you wrote—but never sent—decades ago! Incidentally, that plastic bag is now down to a hefty pound, and new soul-waves keep flooding in, so there could be an L or LX edition in the offing. If you like what's inside LXXXX, stay tuned!

This large an amount of versification is not meant to be read in a few sittings. The ninety—ninety is a celebratory number—selections exist so close to one another on paper that their suddenness of mood and theme change cannot help but distract if read straight through like a Sunday newspaper. After much shuffling and compartmentalizing, I decided to arrange them alphabetically by title and let the quips—and there are some—fall where they may.

My technique may be described as a mixed bag, as it moves from rhyming to free to blank verse, and often to a surprising mix of the three or the unexpected insertion of rhyming couplets at intersections and conclusions. Considerations of style aside, I always attempt to create lyrics rather than mere lines which, despite resembling and being published as poetry, often come across as well-intended and clever but pretentious prose.

In a 2005 New York Times "Poetry Chronicle," an obviously jaundiced critic referred to "the steady-handed competence, ingratiating charm and middle-aged melancholia from which much verse suffers," meanwhile omitting the charm-less, angst-ridden and super-cute. Given such qualitative and tedious burdens, why bother doing poetry? Why not just declare—as I once shamefully did at a book-signing in Boston—that, since WWII, poetry has become an archaic language? Frankly, I had an epiphanous change of heart and mind akin to moving to a blue state from a red state, hence this book is my unlimited-lifetime-warrantee of jubilantly restored faith in the genre.

I must thank my wife Rose Ann for her support and understanding that this collection was a project I absolutely had to finish while time permitted, and for her incisive commentary on poems I brought home from my office to get her opinion on their sense and clarity. In addition, I rather recently acquired the habit of sneaking one or two of these opuses into envelopes containing non-related correspondence to friends and family members, each of whom then enthusiastically encouraged me to stay this course.

Although praise is nice and may well suffice, I have never forgotten my first employer's corny but still useful advisory that "one robin doesn't make a spring."

And now it's too late to guess what he'd say about ninety of them!

Aarpeggio

When you and I are ancient, if we
cannot recall with certainty
what happened yesterday or whether
it made us quarrel or agree,
we may regard our legal tether
as habit's fundamental leather—
a blend of peace and civil war
as reliable as forecast weather—
and love a quaint and distant shore
seen through a porthole or a door.
Or might it seem as fresh as flowers
delivered daily? Ardor like ours
could burn forever if memory has
a more than slowly shrinking mass,
which we won't know 'til we're so old
the difference between heat and cold
might fail to register and we'd go to bed
desiring Tylenol PM instead.

Add Libs

Add to your few fragments
of curious ruin and repair
this autumn leaf flipped over
to show its veined back, its limb
listened to for inner noise—
perhaps an old woods-poem
singing in cellulose vowels;
then add its whole dead tree
as it falls, touching the present
with palsied light-brown hands;
then add these tell-tale fragments
to the fractions of waking time
when small events are captured
as thin, flat, matte, sepia planes
of photographs you've saved
to thumb through, to recall with
the understandable ambivalent joy
of recovering parts of a broken toy.

a/k/a

How to reveal the beauty of this perhaps
    Inanimate device . . . the way it makes
Sunlight an artist, enthralls the lightest touch,
    Arouses wonderment when the heart quakes

Merely from using it for its intention?
    Its vision flutters the senses like a flame,
Causes pens to write, brushes to paint and lenses
    To focus and capture the quarry of good aim.

It has no name nor is it brand-related,
    Being akin to an un-given gift
        Of nebulous color, fashion, heft or size,

But it may be seen and heard and demonstrated
    As a device that even the blind could lift
        And love enough to see their own surprise.

Aperçu

If equal equaled equal, and all was shared
   In standard portions, and nothing private except
One's viscera, and every care was cared
   For by a ministry that keeps the kept;

If every caste was touchable, if races
   Abolished pride's pathetic primitive
Dismay at differences of hair and faces;
   If there was less to own but more to give,

The world would still be round and blue and spinning,
   And man the harassed beast he is today:
Infected with death from the moment of life's beginning,
   Love's lonely stallion selling sweat for hay.

Appearances

Alas, the kingdom of the blind,
    Where Erasmus's one-eyed man is king,
Is universal, even here
    Where vision and freedom are said to ring:

Realm of short-sighted sovereigns,
    And the undecided who look askance,
Who question and who take exception
    Before they blindly countenance.

Look hard! Say, did you ever see
    Such a sorry sight in your half-seen life?
No? Then be here advised the same
    Applies to the regal one-eyed wife.

Monocular am I . . . are you:
Half-sighted, easily seen through.

Avunc

My uncle, well-read gloomy man, emits
    Thick smoke from his cigar and talks of Dickens;
Across the room his wife, my aunt, just sits,
    Shrieks: "Ha!" Sends him a glare that sickens.

Their facing chairs were anchored in this site
    For three decades: hers blue, his brown, both worn;
Even empty they seem poised for a public fight
    Over life's future, present and bygone.

Their bloodless war, which neither side could win,
    Left neither peace nor children in its wake,
And they grew fat, externally and within,
    Feeding upon the flesh of each mistake.

When he had turned his last imprinted leaf,
    While she now settles into her mortification,
That they once loved will remain beyond belief
    To anyone alive at its cessation.

Does every family have casualties like mine,
    Unable to revert to what they were
When eager to send and get a valentine?
    I never asked him. And now I can't ask her.

Bang Lore

Give or take four billion years
    (Earth's imprecise antiquity),
Give a bigger sum for the universe:
    Ten *giga*years older than we!

How could a Koran or a Bible,
    Thirty centuries ago, or less,
Depict a hell-and-heavenly past
    Using more than an educated guess?

Some see us (Man) as accident,
    Others as theophanic plan;
Whichever mind-set you support,
    Brain says: "Confirm it if you can."

Perhaps the planets and their moons
    Were Deus-ex's machination,
Experiments in world-construction
    That failed to match anticipation?

Though I admit to monkey genes—
    Recalling trees climbed and fallen from
Before the scriptures were imagined
    By God or Man or rule of thumb—

I hold this theory about old Bangs:
    Perhaps the cosmos always *was* . . .
And never *wasn't* . . . and we've evolved
    From spacey to serendipitous!

Breathless

Each breath's the subject of demise,
recording the minutes of a meeting
where once again it is acknowledged
you have one less breath to breathe.
But if you *hold* your breath? No matter.
Your disease is, clinically, Time itself
which, even when suspended, ticks
on in silence like the remembered dream
of more being less than it would seem.

Bruises

If a crying child shows you his latest bruise
From tumbling down or wearing too-tight shoes,
This is the soothing unguent you might use:
"I *see* . . . but you'll get over one that small;
There are some others that won't heal at all."
He'll wonder just how high you'd have to fall,
Never guessing you had learned that years ago
When you fell hard for causes he can't know
Or how to see a bruise that doesn't show.

Cicerone

Your *all*, we think, you never gave;
   Some you withheld for future giving:
Not knowing what to serve or save?
   How valuable? When? While you were living?

Some was reserved, a lesser or greater
   Portion of what was once intended
To be made known soon—not now, but later
   In case it had to be amended.

You left us guessing what that might
   Have been, smiling your modest smile
Of a champion watching others fight
   And lose what you had all the while.

When your possessions were accounted,
   The faithful—stricken dumb and blind—
Learned that the residue amounted
   To less than anyone could find.

Cleavage

I split a log, a cut of pine,
And found some golden pitch there, in
So hidden that that stroke of mine
Would miss it if a hair too thin,

And guessed some people I mistrust
Had pitch in them that shone unseen
Beneath their bark's unpolished crust,
Pine-sweet and equally serene.

Then, as I struck the wood once more
And covert nails blunted my blade,
I thought of a girl named Eleanor
Who trusted me, whom I betrayed

By favoring another more endowed,
And a poem I'd started died out loud.

Closet Drama

Your empty clothes hang limply on the rack
    But their scent is crisp and personal and dear;
Their make a stir when touched, then quiver back
    Into their ghostly unfilled shapes. The mere

Suggestion of your breast still lifts that blue
    Dress to the swell of everything hung here,
A penetrating transcendental clue
    You may be elsewhere in the house and near.

It almost seems you shrugged off some of them
    Before they'd time enough to sag or curl,
And they stand preciously on unbent hem
    Like the balanced facts and fancies of a girl.

Consumation

No weakness, citizens: *trash it:*
the packaging, the passé garment,
the cigarette lighter, the camera,
the stamp and coin collection,
the printed news, the ballpoint pen,
the unprinted e-mail, the mono
that should be stereo, the stereo
that isn't digital, the telephone
that can't take pictures, the wife
no longer young, the last five
Levitras (they'll fail to harden
your resolve or levitate hers).
Think you're in consumer heaven
if your wagon won't seat seven?
Frankly, my dear, can you imagine
why you saved little bits of string
and lost your cool if anyone dared
to waste an inch of yellow pencil?
Get with it: *Uncle Sam needs you!*
No shame, the new game's name
is *Riddance*. Why clean or mend
or try to make up with a friend,
or think of fixing something broken?
Dumpster the unrepaired: whatever
you've saved or received as a token
from someone loved or once admired,
and *yourself* the instant you're retired!

Convergence

When you arrive . . . when we first meet,
I cannot guess how we shall greet—
With touching lips, with clasping hands,
Or, each uncertain where he stands,
Weeping or laughing in dismay,
Inclined to vaporize away?
What would you do if I should cry:
"Darling!"—blush, or wonder why?
If you saw other lovers here,
Kissing and keening, O, my dear,
What if those couples stood so tall
We'd miss each other after all?
You might be soon? I might be late?
Apartheid could define our fate?
My hunch, however, is you'll be
Lovely as ever . . . recognizably,
And I, despite my dimmer torso,
Desiring you as much, or more so.

Corporeality

I hate you, O my body, your corpuscles,
growths, lesions, pores, your unpaid
promissory notes which have in truth
made me abhor you since our youth.

Look! Behold this bullied beggar
selling out for life's extension despite
his loss of tactile joy. You're like
a hospital of unmade beds at night,

each of which I try, then rise from—
with a trendy new infection—sadly.
I loath your gift of ease and elegance,
which, like your macular skin, age badly.

The day we were allegedly set free,
I became your helpless captive, numb,
And fed upon until reduced to . . . me,
me, an existential, graying bacterium

on Time's otherwise unspotted linen,
awaiting my hard-earned, too-late terminus,
too aware that during our companionship,
our intercourse, the vicissitude of being us

through health and wellness, wins and losses,
abundance, poverty, trysts and double-crosses,
sighs sighed and operatic groans and grunts,
you've *never* said you love me. No! Not once!

Crazy Lady

"So," you were saying, "there's this crazy lady
who wears black stockings, ballet shoes and bangs:
sixtyish, she feeds the pigeons—where it's shady—
crusts from a Kleenex box, shows yellowed fangs
smiling at a fabulous joke only she could hear.

"Right in the heart of town," you said, "the heart!"
"This city's heartless," I said; "her home is here."
Mother, you're center stage, so play your part!
"Then," as you were saying, "call me a liar
if she doesn't—using as a pillow her carpet bag—

stretch out on Macy's sidewalk like a Buyer
and take a nap!" *Mother, don't move a rag
or trade your reason for some doctor's madness.*
With other true believers, I'll shield your rest
waving a banner reading DANGER . . . GLADNESS!

Cygneture

The moment was a swan
   Glowing whitely as she went
Downstream, sailing on . . . on . . .
   Awkwardly elegant,
Pulling a roiling vee
Of water, passing me,

Pretending I was not
   Her watcher watching there
At his customary spot
   On the river's edge, aware
We'd never spoken or would
If so inclined . . . and could.

For more than fifty years
   We played this cunning game:
The Moment that Reappears.
   The swan? She glows the same,
But—still anticipating
Miracles—I grew old waiting.

Dispositions

Instead of fixing the broken one,
    Strip a replacement from its sleeve:
Pen-refill today, wristwatch tomorrow,
    Your private parts that can't conceive,

Just possibly yourself entire,
    Whether precisely *you* as had
Or five-eyed Igor from deepest space;
    Being immortal . . . is that so bad?

Rather than fill that dead container,
    You burst apart the cellophane
Containing its substitute, and lo!—
    A disposable camera to dispose again.

Since vintage dates from Monday on,
    Forget you cherished Sunday's skin:
Replace it now! You have the con
    So trash what's used . . . plug *New You* in!

Distance

I've come the long way to these truths,
    Lacking the sufferance, the eyes,
The sense, the courage, the way to say
    Them sooner. Now, they materialize

Like magic from a wand, levitate
    And reproduce, as I delight
In freeing slaves and inhibitions
    Enchained by doubts of wrong and right.

History and wealth seem dubious;
    Errors no longer evoke dismay;
Battles need not be waged to win;
    Belief is open to *if* and *nay*.

I came the long way to being able
    To put propriety back in its cage,
Entomb prudence in a cornerstone,
    And learn to master shame and rage.

So now, having read to here, add this:
    Passion can make the fool of you
I was before I found, too late,
    There always was a short way through.

Dobson's Choice

John Dobson, of whom you've likely never heard
    Until this poem (nor I), was a man of science
Whose Big Bang theory will seem absurd
    To those whose dogma, calculus and reliance

Are that billions of years ago—fourteen-point-three—
    Something was made of nothing . . . *our universe!*
Creating everything out of nothing can't be,
    John holds; no cosmic concept could be worse.

Think twice before alleging Dobson's choice
    Implies a pagan view of Genesis.
Think twice (as I have)—doesn't it give voice
    To eternal virgin-birth and synthesis?

What life-span John assigns to heaven and hell
    I cannot say. If they're imagined sites
In his cartography, it's just as well
    Not to assign him maybes, musts, or mights.

Endgame

Down toward its end, life surely
   Is better than this and these;
Toward its nadir, perhaps, its fervor
   Might reawake and please,

Might shriek of starting over
   Like a tree's root—reaching stone—
Exclaims its shocked surprise
   At groping the unknown.

Near its cessation, life might
   Be better for them and those
Who've lived their losing plan
   And permanently pose.

"Might be," I say. But if
   Its close is retrograde?
Well, that's the chance you take,
   The way the endgame's played.

Entr'acte

We read the moment's pregnant silence
as a knock impending but unheard,
as the nanosecond a scheduled union
may be at last about to happen,
as the breathy, wide seductive yawn
of waves about to be withdrawn;

but it shall be breached, the quietude,
as assuredly as heartbeats thump
within their rigid symmetries.
Amid exchanging seasons, in a
limbo noiseless as a frightened thief,
awaiting seed-burst and reborn leaf,

transfigured ratios of gold to gray,
when spring makes icicles discharge
and winter yield its governance,
you sense the dated pause designed
to be discretely slid between
each crack in quartered time, unseen.

This interval has ever been, since
molten matter combined and cooled,
becoming land and air and water,
providing the fragile, balanced power
we've gained the skill to modulate
while losing the will to perpetuate.

Aphonia, lacking lyrics or music,
will stifle our gravid gasping world
should it, untended, rejoin the lifeless
far-flung congeries in godless space.
Pray . . . *pray* this silence quickly breaks,
even with cannonades and quakes!

Evanescence

Love evanesced like last night's rain
Leaving no turbulence or stain,
Not even a scribbled "Bye-bye dear"
To prove love ever had been here,
But it left the mess it always does
When someone says it never was.

Fonetics

In my car (not in my pocket)
gathering dust before I lock it,
though quite compact and unattached
and a source of unity unmatched,
my fone is always switched to *Off.*
To call me: e-mail, wave or cough;
if I don't answer I'm out, I guess;
and the way I love you, I confess,
is *wired* . . . it's never wireless.
See those folks in flux, endlessly talking,
so *On* they're brightly animated,
who can't hang up, even while walking?
Most of their chatterers are unrelated!
They act as if they'll soon be dating,
not going home to someone waiting,
but are they truly communicating
one on one, as they seem to be?
Or pretending there's a he or she
at the other end of the missing wiring?
Or, fearing the solitude of moving
through space and time, merely conspiring
to populate my disapproving?

For Joe at 77

The only sound you could muster,
dying in your favorite heavy chair
while autumn, just outside, colored
your western window's garden view,
watching you like a horrified child,
was a final sticky cough that sought
to utter someone's name or to plead
for help, somehow hovering until it said—
said clearly as an auditor would agree
if present—the following nine words
escaping your throat to collectively
declare: "Peter Pan is dying here alone,
does *anyone* care?" Which should,
when finders find you seated there,
persist in the musty death-room air
as silence capable of being understood.

F-Stop

These my camera saw: the climate
flawless; Time's antique train puffing
to a halt in an old-fashioned station,
its passion now reduced to curly hot air;
saw and recorded alien birdsong
airmailed in messages whose words
were fabulous flummery; and my camera
also observed basic-blue daybreak
without one new life's innocent start
on its solitary wedding march to death,
without a single undeserved demise.
Its glassy fish-eye lens as much as said:
"I see a plaza packed with placid people
on concatenated squares . . . chessmen
awaiting another dubious change of space
beneath the morning moon's pale dead face."
Not that my camera cared, cared whether
this commonplace was more than ordinary
or that it had catalogued current events
compressed and memorized by a brainless chip,
was surely unaware if views inlaid
were false or true, *so* . . . long before those
panchromatic pixels begin to fade,
I am once again compelled to decide
which to reveal, to print, to edit or erase,
and which (if any) of the verities has made
a claim that could or shouldn't be denied.

Genius Thoughts

I marvel at the penetrating flight
Of mind that makes an Einstein out of clay
Like ours *exactly*, yet different as wrong and right.
I could ask Mozart how he got that way,

And Shakespeare why his gift of metaphor
Makes other poets and playwrights seem inept,
But there's no need to wonder . . . they're awake next door
As proof the sleeping great have never slept.

Giggles

Siblings had I three,
Each turned out differently:
None like another . . . or me.

Now think in giga sums:
Six billion people! It numbs
The mind, and I'm all thumbs

Trying to make some sense
Of all this variance—
The why of it, the whence.

Had fate made me like you,
Or you not one but two,
What would life be, love do?

My answer's dry as dust:
Diversity is Man's "must"
If in God's math we trust.

But even an atheist
Can be a realist
On this and won't insist

God be his CPA,
Seeing the gigs in play
Differ as yea from nay.

Grand Dragon

White-garbed, with slit hood-eyes,
it's the late Dr. Green, I presume,
perennial Grand Dragon of more
than one murderous night ride
under the disbelieving stars, who
removed the still-swelling heart
from Quetzelcoatl's virgin
with his keen obsidian scalpel;
who lived to supervise the hanging
of the enchantresses of Salem;
who created Frau Koch out of
mere Nazi propaganda and bits
of folklore. And who is it now
feels for the hated pulse in your
non-Aryan pallid wrist in your
recurrent dream of being guilty
for being you, if not the late
Grand Dragon who survives
in those whose bloodline, skin
or god leaves you out, them in,
justifying the taking of our lives?

Harliquessence

I am not versed in nature's facts, though I
    Behold, take note, consider and rejoice.
What makes her flowers hibernate or die,
    Invokes deep thunder from her quiet voice?
Do not of me ask these, or if I know
    Why the lunar rump (from earth) is never seen,
Or how the moon swings oceans to and fro
    Like an unattended celestial machine.
Ignorant of vitality itself—the cell,
    The seed, the DNA—I cannot tell
If we, like annual plants, ourselves replace,
    Or how life started on this island space.
Still, I pretend to posit why and whence,
    A clown whose act is pratfall eloquence.

Hegira

Beneath his fingers curved around your wrist
    He feels your pulse . . . the flutter that is you,
The will, the urge, the struggle to exist
    Though obviously you're not expected to.

Somewhere a hand that must have felt, at night,
    Your proof of life and silently been glad,
Even if your gentle, flowing quiver might
    Be all of you she actually had—

No, *no*, that's too unkind! Perhaps you were
    Her friend and lover, and a prince of truth.
Let him compose a note and say to her:
    "Yours was a brave and dedicated youth."

Thank God, he'll never know what you've become
    When he moves on, the simple enlisted fetcher
Of what remains of foe and friend, and numb
    To every shriek but: "Corpsman! Hurry! Stretcher!"

Idol Thoughts

Akhnaton had it right:
   One god's enough for the masses.
For a pharaoh he was bright:
   He wore rose-colored glasses

Through which he saw Aton
   As the ultimate chosen deity:
Sans father, sans ghost—the *Sun*
   Whom all could feel and see

In daylight, blazing above
   Field, pyramid and Nile.
Yea, Aton was a god to love;
   Yea, even when his vile

Side surfaced to savage the land
   While he sat there fat and rotary.
Regardless, Akhnaton banned
   Other gods in Egypt's coterie,

Making this pharaoh the first
   To worship a single divinity,
And Aton was far from the worst
   To be worshipped in sole sublimity.

His "Boy King" successor, Tut,
   Whose gods were plural and cool,
Called Akhnaton a sun-burned nut
   Unfit to ordain one-god rule.

Rescinding his edict, Tut said:
   "Our Sun Disc can still be a god,
But only with others, instead
   Of wielding both scepter and rod."

The sun (as some see it) is father
   Of our lonely planet and moon,
Argue the point if you'd rather,
   Say Akhnaton was truly a loon,

But earth can be killed by the sun
   In ten minutes or less, so I say:
Whether fiction or fact, "Sun's the *One*.
   Aton has the con. Let us pray!"

Illuminatus

The slits between closed curtains
and around my bedroom door
are sealed from dawn's faint probe;
as ever, her too-early coming
is presumptuous, unasked for.

So . . . on I doze, granted one more
asymmetric dream of yore,
another unfinished two-act play
authored by suspended animation
in many-hued invisible ink.

Dawn's feeble incandescence
fingers my manufactured chattel
(quilt, books, carpet, paintings)
as if marveling at how cleverly
those dark dumb things were made.

Then . . . *presto!* I sense time left
for sickness / health / hope / despair
to work further ephemeral magic
with my present's quick white rabbit
and future's collapsible black hat.

Inamorata

You asked for this, one special ode
In rhyming couplets for the road
To eternity we're strolling on,
To read aloud, to smile upon.
Know that our home is full of you
When you're on some rendezvous
And miles away from me and it,
I see you gesture, walk and sit
As if at arm's length, hand's length, finger's,
Your essence having mass and lingers.
Despite what other poets claim,
Presence and absence are not the same:
Nonresidence (no need to ponder)
Could never make my heart grow fonder.

Indiana

A good first toy, small,
for any boy, this pliant
red india-rubber man.
Stretched to full span
he snaps to normal size;
any boy might hear, with
pleasure, even surprise,
his memorably decorous
fast flatulent *pffi!* Prise,
gouge or tread on him:
see scars disappear, see
flesh forget. Dropped,
squeezed, twisted, see
india man smile, shrug
uncompressed and heal
like water cut with a knife.
A good first toy, a man
not to live like or follow,
but any boy (any girl) can
if adaptable and hollow.

Investiture

"Commit and you live,
conceal and you die,"
my soul warns again
regardless that I
hear it so often
and never reply.

It might have said to
my "Why?" (long ago),
"You have goods to offer,"
"don't you dare show?"
Yes, *I do*, but I've feared
hearing "No."

Junction

The sky was use-worn as an old blue quilt,
The sheen and puffiness frayed out of it,
And, leaking frowsy cotton, seemed to wilt
To less than the space it was supposed to fit.

The line of mountains sagged and hunkered down,
Reduced to uplands of subnormal height;
Denver, below, was an empty, haunted town,
Its ghost the only humanoid in sight.

And there we sat in the front seat of my car,
Silent, not touching, watching worsening weather
Diminish a love affair we'd driven too far
When broken for us to put it back together.

Who would speak first? Resign? Confess? Deny?
You had the guts, Eileen . . . it wasn't I.

Kinethics

If you have wondered why divisions split
The family of mankind into cliques and sects
Which obviously cannot tolerate each other
Despite equivalent souls and intellects,
And why such carnage transpires because of it
And will until God ends what He began:
Ashamed of sharing a homely common mother,
Fratricide is their instinctive master plan
For silencing kin who dare to cry out "Brother."

Last Rites

The locusts are swarming and
angry at this unseasonable time;
the sky is soiled with locusts, their
song louder than panicked women.

The rats are swarming with a new
uncommon courage, fur to fur
making an immense gray costume
sized to envelop our emerald planet.

Hungry and heartless, they must
devour our books, our formulae,
our deeds and wills and contracts,
our histories. Then we shall hear

a sucking sound much like the
last sweet water in drainpipes,
as our treasured few moist meters
of arable earth swirl by us into

the unlit acrid sump of space, as
all the rats and locusts lift their
tiny faces to ours for death's hot,
parched, excruciating final kiss.

Leavings

No, not for me,
    Nor for my nation
A destiny
    You'd call Salvation,

Surely not Heaven
    And surely no Hell
To grace or leaven
    What the stars foretell:

That even when less
    Became more, our story
Would limn distress
    Louder than glory,

And show our souls
    Strewn deep in space
As faint black holes
    And commonplace,

And find deliverance
    In the now and here
Come only once
    Each just-passed year.

Lettitude

Let fade or flourish, set or shine the moon,
    But let our secrets shimmer in its dust;
Let us aspire to the future soon
    Because the living surely may and must.

Let them deride who laugh the most of all.
    Let every language be obscure which is.
Let noisy climbing be the sound of fall
    If theirs be misdirected business.

The host that marches in the dark of day . . .
    Let it be untranslatable as static.
Let time deceive itself as to the way
    We measure lapses in the enigmatic.

Life or Death

Poised between being and non-being,
you need a certain weight of will to live . . .
remain *alive*, I mean. How much—a gram,
a dram, a milliwatt, a measure of heft
the calculus of variation cannot explain?

You try to estimate the proper mix of what
it is that keeps spines vertical instead of prone,
brains evaluating touch and go, and pride
and love replaying the adagio movement
of your nocturne until their fingers bleed.

When that old tyrant (your father? mine?)
last laughed he sounded like a toy balloon untied
as the lower globs of phlegm replaced the top . . .
yet, even so, a neutron of vital force remained!
Can you explain away such feckless continuity?

Defeated in some high-tech enterprise, mortified,
your brilliant youth with nothing left but penury
and eighty kilograms of curdled chemistry
shops for a new razor and a spray deodorant,
willing himself tomorrows against his wish.

Madam, having lost husband, child and pet
to the Hummer that totaled their Chevvy SUV,
now plans to cope, seeing on her mirrored lips
the smile behind the sylph who was, and, yes,
the widowed college beau who still telephones.

How to face the order and obligation v. oblivion,
sickbed and chemicals v. escape? To set
parameters for entropy v. acceptance, or trust
your smoothbore to say "Enough's enough"
and loudly, should the staying get too tough?

Little hitler

In some well-hidden corner of your mind,
    Despite your lore, your faith, your common sense,
Because I am not kindred of your kind
    You hate me without contrition or pretense.

No need for masks; no residue of doubt . . .
    Your little hitler despises me forever.
When it seems virtuous to vote him out,
    Either you waver or he is too clever,

Hiding until the polls are almost closed,
    Then coldly scrawling X beside my name.
And where's my anger? Why am I disposed
    To rationalize *you're* not the one to blame,

That in your so-called "bringing up," a hitler
    Was psychosocially bred into you?
(You were unaware because adolph was littler,
    And you weren't born a Gypsy or a Jew.)

Where *is* my anger? A challenge worthy of
    More questioning than I've time left to answer,
And my own führer—when push came to shove—
    Had seven lives left after dying twice from cancer.

Lou

My father sits in a bright corner,
tanning in the late October sun,
where perished leaves flutter down
like dollars thrown from a window;
they gasp around his feet, already spent.
At other times, leaf-fall is brown paper
tassels and swirls—confetti left over
from yesterday's passed parade.

Warming in my mortgaged corner
of the seasons, nature's molting
quite like his own (having dignity
despite a future as detritus to be
burned or buried or blown into
other dying fields), he sits shirtless,
thinking winter thoughts, saying
"I am still here; I don't know why."

A proper positive person with real
dismays and mortifications, with
strenuous convictions seldom shared
by those as close to him as kin,
he suns today in the shed of trees
(though I have moved away,
though we were never close), man and site
as had . . . still there. I don't ask why.

Love-in

Some day you'll find
 My slender book:
"A Deposition."
 Then, as you look
Through, in a peace
 Between defeats,
Try to hear *me*
 Among its sheets.
If it's incomplete,
 My brief résumé,
I might have had
 Some more to say
But—not enough time?
 One book (very thin)
That leaves hate out
 And leaves love in.

Made Things

Consider the wonderment of man-made things
accepting nature's heady silent challenge to
"use me if you can"—shiny invented things
recording her prodigal variety, telling her hours,
repairing her faithful belligerent wounded billions,
switching on and off her incandescent powers,

combining coincidences far beyond probability.
Consider things fashioned for lowering and lifting,
precisely redesigned from previous imprecisions,
things whose half-life may be the millisecond
between aim and shoot, things both willfully or
casually made for purposes not fully reckoned;

consider the uses of so many things made from
earth's myriad 'given' asymmetries and fragments,
then wonder why their benefits went horribly wrong
in timing, distribution, application, and deadliness
that sucked the music from ephemeral evensong
even before its immateriality had time to evanesce.

Manhattan Serenade

The City stirs, feeling its private parts
    manipulated by unloving blind
masseurs, as if aware that nothing starts
    without fanfare or until a touch that's kind;

and then it suffers disparate spurts of sound
    with ever shorter silences between
them until, finally, no silence may be found
    even scores of feet below what's paved or green.

The City wakes to scurryings and scrapes;
    its folks accrete like a self-linking chain
until their once-clean differentiated shapes
    merge to become a singular spreading stain.

Arising from uneasy, fear-shortened sleep,
    having dreamed of drowning in liquescent air,
the City reprises its terrible urge to keep
    today from happening—here, or anywhere.

Matter Natter

Does it really matter if Dark Matter—
the sub-luminous sea of energy
comprising some ninety-nine percent
of our antique expanding cosmos—
is divisible invisible fragmentation?
Particles deemed possibly neutrinos
whose mass approaches naught or nigh?
Or if this vast and darkling deep
is hot or cool, or awake or asleep?

Does it matter if the cosmic solid stuff—
red dwarfs, interplanetary junk,
stars, stardust, asteroids, black holes—
comprises merely a puny perverse
point-zero-five percent of the Universe?
Or that no one living truly knows
if Dark Matter *is* what fills time's sky;
if its ubiquitous clay (like Earth's)
is peopled by beasties who multiply?

Regardless, we go about our business
not knowing what a substance is
that's more transparent than love's passion;
that's possibly divine; that invests us
with a fugue of silent music . . . a stuff
whose specific gravity may be nil?
Dark Matter resides where nothing will,
filling the space between hither and yon
like a midnight dream you can count upon.

Messy Antics

Today I suddenly wondered why
    A messiah is needed or expected.
"To save us," you say. For what? From what?
    Why someone old or resurrected?

A savior from the here and now
    Would likely be (in my opinion)
Better prepared to lead us forth
    Unto that loftier dominion;

A leader keen on computer protocol
    And daunting digital devices,
One who can fix them when they're broken
    And cheerfully defray their prices.

But if it's too late for our deliverance,
    If *homo sap.* can soar no higher
And life gets ever longer on a world
    Doomed not to end in ice or fire

(Which seems both fact and fantasy)
    Your messianic dialectic
Then seems to be more creditable
    And mine transparently dyspeptic.

Meum et Tuum

Below, an empty page to register your Tomorrow,
    Or someone's odyssey of his Before;
Here future and history will be truly written
    When time permits, when there's no metaphor

To enhance reality and mask its scars.
    On this blank leaf only hard words survive.
Untruths erase themselves: they leave no trace
    Of life so burdened it scarcely was alive.

I do not write myself upon this paper
    For fear of penning self-erasure there:
My errant thoughts, my use of nights and days,
    And much I might have done if not aware

That a lifetime is its own unpublished scribe,
    Indifferent to piety, failure or success.
Here, take this wordless virgin page! See what
    Remains after you tell but don't confess.

Mind's Eye

Flying west from seaside Boston,
    Looking out and down where mostly tree
And river prevail, I saw, instead,
    A countryside of property,

Of deeds, liens, contracts, living wills,
    A paper quilt of ownership
Covering America coast to coast,
    Its islands to their farthest tip.

There had been other flights on which
    I gloried in silky clouds flown through,
The stubborn thrust of mountains, in towns
    Flown over and cemeteries, too . . .

But not this time! This time I heard
    The shuffle of documents, the cough
Of lawyers; I saw receipts prepared
    And owners signing on and off.

Between the self and the façade
    That make you *you* until you die,
I may find such vision and revision
    The next time you're what I overfly.

Mishima

Your vision was the hostile shape of
cherished things (the crookedness
of straight, the wideness of narrow) as
you waited and watched, anticipating
the ultimate victim you had so keenly
limned, waiting for him to finish
your denouement, tired, already dying
of acute November and its cure. *Hai,*
given no choice, Yukio, we read your
verdict as justified . . . as well-deserved
as living is to those on time's small page
who cannot not parse your larger rage.

Miss Tique

Where have you been since I last asked?
    (*No answer.*) What have you done since then?
(*Silence.*) Were I to guess: Saks Fifth?
    The MOMA? Gone to Europe again?

To further guess—well, frankly, I
    Don't care to. You're a made-up person,
Not real . . . a QWERTY woman with whom
    Intimacy would only worsen

An affair; let ours be platonic, breathless
    And imagined! The truth and gist of it
Is this: I saw you enter that taxi,
    Coat, skirt and legs swishing a bit,

Evoking more unanswered questions:
    Going where . . . to whom? Your face and hair
Preceded you unseen, and now
    I guess I see them everywhere.

Muni Bonds

If you have ever lived a city
   You cannot live a smaller place
With nothing and no one to fear or pity,
   No walls or busses to deface,

No twitching signs, no dusty trees
   With pigeons exiting and mating in,
No swirling subway-scented breeze
   To make butts, cans and wrappers spin.

Once you have truly lived a city
   Down to its sour, nightmare ends,
Where drunks define the nitty-gritty
   And strangers wink at you like friends,

Where a shop like Tiffany's seems closed
   To you as if it breathes a different air,
And yours is the name nobody knows
   Or wishes to, well . . . you don't care

Because you love it like your mother
   And, despite its siren-shrieks and stir,
If a bar-girl there says "Howdy, Brother,"
   The odds are even you can sleep with her.

Nachtmusik

The verse he quickly drafts tonight,
May, by the morning's fickle light,

Let slip its rhythm, dissolve like ice,
Or bore like madrigals sung twice.

At midnight's noon, when shadows dazzle,
Your laird emerges from your vassal

To set his breathlessness to rhyme
Exalting new and just-passed time.

Thoughts flow as fast as fleeing elves
And almost seem to write themselves.

Though swift and glib, his poetry
Could be a bell that rings for thee,

For if wood can be a violin,
Words also may have music in.

Obiter Dicta

Two friends are said about to die,
    So truth or rumor flies apace
As bad news always does, and I
    Have no one able to replace

His gift or her amazing grace.
    Now the ranks close on my goodbye:
Here a firstborn, there a new face,
    Strange name, wry smile, appraising eye.

If they've consumed their time and space,
    Why grieve, why reminisce or sigh?
You sense their quarry deserved the chase
    And what they craved was worth the try.

Life's metrics quickly quantify:
Deaths divide . . . survivors multiply.

On State Street

I used to race the marble of its stairs,
    Whirling on brazen cherubs at the turns,
Breath hissing, like steam in radiators did,
    As I sped past mahogany panels, and urns

Whose further side was hidden like the moon's,
    And under gilded, scalloped ceiling heights
That seemed almost too churchlike for a place
    Where barristers told clients their legal rights,

Where bootblacks polished shoes and barbers trimmed,
    And elevators were run by ladies who numbered
The approaching floor and smiled as if they knew
    I was too young to work there and unencumbered.

The last time I returned to Boston and looked,
    The building had been demolished . . . *wasn't there!*
Had died a pauper's death, perhaps like Mozart,
    Loved only by lovers who remain aware.

Outgrowth

There must be poetry in hair,
The stuff grows on us everywhere,

Even, it's claimed, for many an hour
Post mortem, after brains lose power

To cogitate, hearts cease to beat,
And flesh can't shrink from cold or heat.

Whatever the color, curl or site,
Hair's programmed to arise at night

and prowl—like dreams of bawdy places—
Through porous pates, backs, legs and faces;

And, wanted or not, however bare
The spot, it strives to settle there.

Some day I'll find that song within
The filaments . . . come thick or thin!

Past Imperfect

The old man is dying in his tousled bed,
Thoughts caroming inside his old forehead

Like a storm of wings as he reckons whether
The next gray flutter is the final feather

Of a bird that will never see trees again;
He's thinking: Who, what, where, why, when,

And his mind is blurred and bleak and busy
As the faces around him, eyes saying: "Is he—"

When one, vaguely familiar in the way
Owls resemble people, asks: "—better today?"

Pathology

Pathways are seldom laid where people walk;
    They square the corners feet would rather cross
And lengthen shorter travel lines as if
    Some wasted time is not an actual loss.

A judgment path goes only where it's laid;
    Its paved or pebbled trail will hew the line
Drawn quickly by draftsman on a print
    Subordinating desire to design.

An impulse path is never laid or covered;
    It wanders with the coming and the gone
Having no respect for property or signs
    Because it's usage-made for walking on.

Some like a path defying law and order,
    The route from A to Z and all between,
Regardless of what perils they encounter
    Or any fool who dares to intervene.

Though "laid" means fixed and "made" means flexible,
    Don't bet on either one except to change;
Most any path that leads you down familiar
    May well, on coming back, return you strange.

Picture Perfect

The blind dream of color,
    The deaf dream of sound,
The weak dream of power,
    The lost being found.

The slave dreams of freedom,
    The leader of losing,
The lame dream of motion,
    The gambler mischoosing.

The poor dream of assets,
    No matter how small,
Because hoping is better
    Than no dream at all.

And what do I dream of,
    Having lived a life longer
Than some twice my age
    Who once seemed stronger?

The same as I wished for
    When I was a child:
Kept secrets, shared magic,
    The call of the wild,

Not life after death
    But a full one before,
And to have all my limbs
    At the end of the war.

The maimed dream of wholeness,
   The sick dream of health,
The rich dream of keeping
   Their descendants in wealth.

If you have a dream
   Whose reality doubles
In the still of the night
   And pleasures or troubles,

Don't tell me its meaning
   Unless you've a mind to,
For I've a new dream
   And I'm not inclined to.

Position Paper

Progress, to each of us, meant a different gait,
    A disparate way, a diverse destination;
Since *down* to me was *up* to you, the date
    And place we'll next meet bogs my calculation,

Leaving to mere chance a future intersect
    Perhaps as vain as love we tried before,
Which I thought gainsaid by your intellect,
    You by my rush to lay you on the floor.

Shall we reprise that drama, if or when
    Our orbits accidentally re-cross?
Would you (as I suspect) become again
    The Pyrrhic victor who deplores her loss?

Rethinking the sweets of *my* ascendancy:
They've more than slightly soured on the tree.

Prime Time

I often ponder on our prime
Which, through the restive roil of time,
Is thought to be in lovelier shape
Than when we more resembled ape
Or gamboled in Mesozoic grime.

How were we when the mammoth was,
Or when we soared or swam or slid?
I long to know what ugly did,
After observing what handsome does
And finding it less than fabulous.

Psalmsung 23

Yea, though I walk
   Through the valley of death
I'm empowered to talk
   When I catch my breath.

It restoreth my soul
   To keep love so nigh
Its ultimate goal
   Shineth whitely nearby.

Yea, afar on still water
   I am never alone
Since I righteously bought her
   A wireless phone.

When I flew to Tahiti
   To achieve singularity,
I heard: "Be good, sweetie,"
   With digital clarity.

Connection extends
   To mine enemies, too,
Though I maketh amends
   They seldom get through.

He prepareth me well—
   By His edict of stricture—
For the shadow of Hell
   In her telephone picture.

Yea, the Lord now denies
   Me the joy of the olden
Implicit replies
   That made silence so golden.

Quantum Leap

Were all our elements to scatter
Like dust between the stars, no matter.
Our sums are fixed in mass and motion;
Their "nothing" is a fictitious notion.

When you rejoin me where I wait
You cannot be a moment late
Regardless of the time, the season,
The passage taken, the speed, the reason.

That place will be the perfect site
For resurrection, day or night,
In space, on earth, or it may be
Fission or fusion—any degree.

Yet, should we fail to coincide
In ways or means here specified,
All atoms being contiguous
What touches either touches us.

Quarterly Report

The months of summer I love most of all:
Their plentitude of sunlit noons; the tall

Green silk-wrapped corn; immodest memories
Of loving whom and why and what I pleased;

The sear of sand beneath bared feet; the sheen
Of grass; the look of bodies tanned and lean.

Time was I rated spring as somewhat better,
Once prayed for snow like a long-awaited letter

Or the color turn of autumn leaves. Why those
Sweet seasons soured? Good question! I suppose

Warmth's what I really crave—more heat, less change,
And none I've truly loved will find that strange.

Quintessence

I cannot see close-to to thread a needle,
   Or read my will, or push a key straight in.
This page resembles something under water—
   A paper fish that's neither thick nor thin.

And so it goes with over-fifty eyes,
   Not to mention other aging hits and misses.
In truth, I haven't dipped into the Bible
   Since my last date's last sweetly-given kisses,

Except King James' version in Hilton's drawer
   When I was book-less and despised TV.
(Since learning keys have smooth and craggy edges,
   Unlocking doors comes easier to me.)

Poor vision at fifty, though I still do verse,
Has made its dazzle dim and lightness worse.

Quotidian

Didn't open the mail,
    Didn't answer the phone,
Failed to solve any problems—
    Homo sap.'s or my own.

Nothing new in the news,
    Nothing bright on the tube,
Not a book to peruse.
    Now I felt like a boob

Since none of my causes
    Had viable reasons.
The garden was drab
    As it gets between seasons.

Our attack on Iraq
    Was foundering badly,
As it had in Viet Nam—
    As reckless, as sadly.

A day of depression?
    No, a day of thanksgiving
With tomorrow drawn near
    As the dead to the living.

Summation

More than the sum of all your parts
    Are you, am I, are we. Their sum
Is Einstein's formulaic *m;*
    His *e* is what we have become

After unequal ebbs and starts,
    Adding an essence truly ours
And as far removed from sight or touch
    As fragrance from the stuff of flowers.

When seeking love in opened hearts
    That surgeons struggle to repair,
Blood, flesh and bone may be observed,
    But love's transparent even there.

Your mirror, clothes and photograph?
Mere show and tell. Much less than half!

Rondo

I thought of making a small collection of words for you . . .
Then I thought *no*, something purposely short would never do.

An epic refrain of parts of speech might contain too many.
And today my poor pen became inkless before penning any.

Let this elegy, laded with love's last phrases that never got written,
Suffice as an idyll, too, and deliver the quick to the smitten.

Seascape

The ocean, gravestone cold if some touched you,
    Seeks warm residuum to slide between;
Its farther swell is purple, the nearer blue;
    As it ascends the beach, foam-splattered green.

That breathless sigh is tide's half-gasp, half-suck
    And mild surprise at how the coastline tasted.
With hungry shrieks, a gull swoops down to pluck
    A risen fish before the waves displace it.

The sky's an azure vault with pop-art clouds.
    The scene is bathers, boats and rock-rimmed grit.
Girls shyly shed their jeans and cotton shrouds
    To gild the pelt and flaunt the best of it.

My camera digitalizes what it sees.
    I ponder which to print, which to delete:
The fish? The girls? The sea? If none of these,
    Perhaps I'll leave this poem incomplete.

Second Coming

Were I reborn containing all I know
    Now, as a man, I'd be no less confused
Or happier; facts are not things that grow
    By being added to. I've been well-used

By innate gifts and incapacities,
    And doubtless would come to me all over if I'd
Another go at life and time with these
    Few assets and no more smoldering inside.

Mine is a light that should eventually fail,
    And, being out, stay out. Isn't darkness good?
But if I must come back, make me a frail
    Fantastic foreign flower in a wood

Where, blooming drowsily beneath each sun,
    I might become (at last!) the most fertile one.

Sequence

Clean set of prints upon the night's new snow
Publishing paragraphs of heel and toe,
Explaining where they had a mind to go
Despite anyone's rejection. This crisp parade
Suggests their scrivener was unafraid
To walk alone: the concavities he made
Say he'd confronted danger before and knew
His way even when whited-out from view,
The same as lovers, dogs and seasons do.
If, following that direction, hoping to see
His denouement, you may find it winterly
Too . . . unlike the warm reunion it could be.

Skyfall

In 2003 the sky again came down
in fiery fragments sharp as knives,
asymmetric lead-edged shards of
old stained glass shaken loose from high
rose windows, a shower of disciples,
crosses, saints and shattered scripture
that clattered numerously, flashing by
in untranslatable bytes of text
unable to save one soul from hell.
The skies come down whenever peace
is threatened . . . their rainbows shatter,
the firmament becomes the enemy,
as thirty centuries of history has shown,
which those ordaining should have known.

Stardom

Far out in the translucent cool of space
   The fires of dead and dying stars still burn,
Proving the passion of their time and place
   To us who make the heavens our concern;

Even when they have absolutely perished
   They tell their casualty in living light.
How then to know for sure the one you cherished
   Was really *there* when you looked up that night?

Stet

Gone frail with age, and these to show for it:
Each pain a bullet needing to be bit;
Leisure unasked for; clothes that used to fit;
Quotidian change you'd rather not admit;

Some sore, some useless parts; the need to sit.
What good remains to show for all of it?—
Perhaps a torch passed down; a will well writ;
Insurance to recompense your family's hit;

The character to silently submit
To the nonplus of deliquescent wit,
While awaiting the end of what seemed infinite
Before you glimpsed the pendulum and the pit.

How now brown cow—fight fiercely on, or quit?
Me! *Time?* I'll never live too much of it!

Streamlines

Life's watercourse is never just one way
but first downstream, then back, then up again,
sometimes transformed into an angry spray,
then winding calmly back to where you stand,
pretending it's the same neat multiplicand
that passed by you a day or year ago.
It often gyrates like a victim of vertigo,
bleeds loudly around and over stone, then mends
its lesions with transparent skill and ends
most evenings being pretty much contained
between the banks it was supposed to flow
in molecules less chaotic than ordained.
The rules, however, were custom-made for breaking,
giving water at least one chance to flow uphill
and run a risk that's possibly worth taking
when time permits and it is standing still.

String Theory

The banjo and the mandolin . . .
Have they stepped aside or just given in
To something new? No? What's the score?
I seldom hear them anymore.

Now add the lyre, post horn, and lute . . .
What silenced them but left the flute?
Where are the organ-grinder and
His simian partner with cap in hand?

Has anyone written (except me)
An elegy for the calliope,
The shawm, the Jew's harp or the zither?
If gone indeed, I wonder whither.

Ten O'clock News

Crises compose the idiot tune I tune to,
    Their sight-read music every night renewed,
Importantly phrased as if for me alone,
    No fugue or movement left to be construed;

I watch a face lip-synch for thirty minutes,
    Mouthing today's sextet of broken things:
At ten, a rhapsody on a theme of terror,
    A threnody of crime and toppled kings;

I dare not sleep for fear of missing the turn
    From bad to worse, or the mind-set of a seer
Who already knows the song but will rehearse
    Until the switch to advertising beer.

Although disaster orchestrated nightly
    Affords some pleasure from faraway effects,
It does provide a pause for a cadenza
    Of almost newsworthy conjugal sex.

The Look

The old look you wore like a moustache . . .
the look that said "been there, done that,"
the look of unsophisticated schadenfreude
that curled the thin pink line of mouth into
an antonym of charity, then silently added
wry sweetness to your catalogue of imitation . . .
well, I never did forget it, not even when
you took a one-way trip to heaven, assuming
(I did!) that hell was over-booked just then.
Now, my most agnostic reader is a confessor,
forced to conceal the look of your successor.

Tidings

All my life the poets have been dying:
my life is instances of writers silenced
and tucked away in unfamiliar ground
before their time, like golden tick-less watches
awaiting patiently to be rewound.
This April won't blossom Eliots or Lowells,
or Plaths or Cummings, or even a McLeish,
merely tulips reciting simple prayers
in language far less musical than theirs.
My life is filled with poets perishing early
after sculpting chaos into what we are;
bards who dared the dark and dangerous;
who could extract the fire of a star
and make it flame so famously in us;
whose interludes were incompletely lived;
who learned the art of tolerance too late,
and the art of loving too well to tolerate.
For giving less than giving all, their best
drifts on in future time like notes in bottles
that will never touch a shore or come to rest.

Time Frame

Once time was worn so thin
I saw tomorrow through its trees,
scarlet, white, hairless
as little-boy bloodied knees.

I saw it morph to indigo,
the blue denim with a splotch
and bits of future riveted
like stars along its crotch.

I heard the minutes jump,
utter "Yep!" audibly,
and promise progress without
a tick of specificity.

If I forget when time
was thin as bandage gauze
through which unhealed wounds
were visible, it's not because

I disremember seeing it
or flinching at the thought
of time not evolving
into what was sought.

Timelines

I would be brief and edgy, sure
as a second-hand nearing midnight,
making this poem of sixteen-lines
precise, its lyrics perfect, pure,
persuasive, memorable as wine's
last statement, love's first stolen kiss
when a sudden aria of breeze
serenades the fugitive who is seized.

I would be unabridged but focused
and inclusive as I deliver Then's
uncensored stylus onto Now's
wide-open, noteless notebook, penning
fluent passages in fresh
dark dales and hills of English verse
before the noisy dawn replaces
my song with lengthy lesser graces.

Trinity

Three are the times
   I said I love you:
Once yesterday
   Two times today,

Never intending
   To mean "pro tem,"
Less than "I do,"
   Or threaten "nay."

Now every saying
   Finds love changed,
A new amount
   To add and pay;

Even so, whatever
   The magnitude
Its sum is two:
   One size . . . one way,

Reshaped to fit
   The moment's fugue.
Just as a sculptor
   Thumbs his clay

To make from want
   A thing beloved,
I juggle three words
   My heart says: "Say!"

Ventilation

I've never seen the wind but I can sense
Its strength, direction and velocity,
And clearly hear its voice across immense
Distances (wordless in the future tense).
Its push can lift a skirt or fell a tree
Or cause The Times to fly far left of me.

Wind can, when so disposed, be almost mute,
Submissive as a voice in private prayer,
As a lover just proposed to, as hanging fruit,
As music wafted through a silver flute,
Then suddenly evoke—transfusing air—
Hostility, and the need to twist and tear.

Having never truly seen it, only its play
With things (often fumbling as if blind),
I'm flabbergasted when I hear you say:
You think you've never "seen" wind blow this way.
Wind is unseen! By now I'm half-inclined
To view it simply as a state of mind.

Wasteland?

The earth, somehow reborn each April,
   Is not productive everywhere:
You can observe where living ends
   And roots can't probe another layer.

Above and down to unseen depths,
   Life recreates itself outside,
Supporting the claim that it is able
   To reverse the death of what has died.

One poet (Eliot) found the season cruel,
   Another (Chaucer) called "Aprille" sweet.
Concerning demise and restoration,
   The greatest minds shall never meet,

So why do our simple minds still cling
   To hopes of attaining immortality?
I'm not a tree, *you're* not a flower,
   Nor are we ever going to be!

Weekdaze

Monday seemed to go like these:
the mindless loop dogs trot;
the exodus of birds disturbed;
the wind both sides of stillness;
a stack of letters left unopened;
stanzas ending with prepositions
(in. on. under. to.), left unfinished
for art to live in undiminished.

As panicked as squirrels neared,
as furtive as cats picked up to pet
and gray as cerebella, Tuesday arrived
like a stretch limo with no one in it,
which, when investigated, I found
not newsworthy but curious—the
poem Wednesday might dedicate
to someone willing to translate.

Western-449

If I'm to die today by accident—
the crash of this prop plane flying
low, Reno to Sacramento, flown
over snow, spruce, graven stone,
thin crooked glittery rivers and
tessellated interstate, let it be now
in May beneath whose hazy sphere
no sound (but Western-449)
survives the frigid air outside. Here
I feel safe . . . warm as an unborn
child able to contemplate a future.

Should 449 explode, burn, curl
its guts into a tsunami of fluids,
carpets, toilet seats, backpacks,
papers, and panicked passengers,
let my destination be high, wide
as the timberline of a mountain top,
where what is left of me can see
its discontinued self wing on
in flights that don't arrive or stop,
my soul intact, transparently
good to (and after) its last drop.

Whispers

(Quote from Thomas Hornsby Ferril)

"I can look at an axle in a sage arroyo, and
hear them whispering, the back-seat lovers
. . . starting something over." And I hear them,
too . . . the dying, the dead, of American wars
needless and undeclared; and the maimed
who never fully live, love or can be loved,
whispering the way sad minds communicate
at night, considering if waning gratitude is
enough pier and beam to structure a life upon,
using the fewest words—*why*, repeated.
Our casualties may be heard intimating like
wind blowing back to its nativity from around
fallow fought-over earth, bearing already-old
news of how the pious faithful have hated
one another—fanatically, fatally, forever.
Even without your hearing aids, you hear
them whispering their painful truths; even
lacking foresight or hindsight, you see
the tombs, urns, crosses, prostheses, and see
the one-legged one-eyed young kings, the
name among graven names of each whose
dream of starting something over crashed
and burned. Daily, hourly, clearly I hear them
(surely among the millions am not unique)
and offer, brief as it is, stanzaic hope that
even *one* someone in the front-seat of affairs
of governance hears, relents, and truly cares.

Zero-Sum

Advancing age wipes clean, smoothes out, fills in
   Time's cracks; it fails to notice what is stained,
Which, years ago, it might have railed against
   Despite some risk and nothing to be gained.

So don't ask me to say why You are You . . .
   Whether Creationism is right or nutty . . .
If Darwin's Theory is a ladder or a trap . . .
   Is Sex still sin when you're no longer rutty . . . .

Now senior, I'm one whose hindsight's twenty-twenty.
   I know what you have done, and I, and those
Who did much worse. Do you wonder why the young
   Don't do it better? Devolution, I suppose.